© 2021 English Masterclass

All rights reserved. No part of this publication may be reproduced, in any form or by any means, without prior permission in writing of the author.

This Book Belongs To:

....

Quick tips to help you use this book:

1. Read your chosen question very carefully

2. Highlight or <u>underline</u> key words

3. Plan your main ideas and the overall structure

4. Use a wide range of vocabulary

5. Remember to use accurate grammar, spelling and punctuation

6. Finally, you may start with any question in this book!

Happy Writing!

Everyone grumbled. The sky was grey. We had nothing to do and nothing to say ...

Continue the story.

"Mum! Mum! I don't feel very well. I don't think I should go to school today." "What's the matter, Tom? Have you got a pain in your tummy again?"

Continue the story.

One evening, Ben stepped outside for a quick breath of fresh air, after giving his mother her supper ...

Continue the story.

Write a letter to a friend in Germany who has never been to England before. Tell her what your school is like, what subjects you study and what activities you do.

Try to make your letter as interesting as possible.

Write a letter to a cousin, inviting them to spend a holiday at your home with your family.

Sarah was standing by the small river looking at the stepping stones. There was a large round stone, a pointed one and a flat grey one in the middle ...

Continue the story.

Tom was awakened early next morning by the happy singing of birds. The sun was streaming through his bedroom window and everything looked so bright ...

Continue the story.

The children waited outside the door for a long time. It was getting dark. Then they heard footsteps inside the house ...

Continue the story.

Write a letter to a friend who is in hospital.

Write a story about a family who has an exciting adventure on a desert island.

Write a story about a great escape.

Imagine you are a butterfly. Describe a day in your life.

Should school children wear uniform? What do you think?

Write about a day you spent in London with your family.

If you were allowed to travel on your own by plane to visit a country of your choice, where would you go to and why?

You and your sister have decided to prepare a special birthday meal for your Mum.

Describe what you are going to cook.

Write a description of a place that you do not like. Please explain why you do not like this place.

Write clear instructions for your grandmother on how to use a mobile telephone.

If you are given £100 and you are allowed to spend it on anything you like, what would you buy?

Write about a school trip that you really enjoyed.

Write a diary entry about what you did at school yesterday.

Imagine you could be invisible for a day. What would you do? What places would you visit?

Invent a new gadget for cleaning the house. Describe this gadget and write a set of instructions to help the user.

Write a letter to your best friend who has recently moved to a new school.

Pretend it is your birthday next Saturday. Write the text for a party invitation which you will be sending to your friends.

You and your friends are going on a shopping trip in a big town. Describe how you are feeling and what you are hoping to buy.

Write a letter to your cousin who lives in a different country, telling him about yourself, your school and the town where you live.

Tom and Jack are brothers. One day, they decide to prepare a special meal for their parents.

What did they cook? What did their parents say?

Describe an interesting adventure you had with your family last summer.

What is the funniest book you have ever read? Describe what you found particularly funny in this book.

Can you think of a few things that would make your neighbourhood better? Write an article to persuade people to do these things in order to improve your neighbourhood.

If you could meet one character in any of the books you have read, who would it be and why?

Dogs make better pets than cats. What do you think?

Write a clear description of the oldest person you know.

What is your favourite cartoon character? Describe this character so that the reader can understand why you like them so much.

A new pupil is going to join your class next week. Write a letter to them describing your class so that they can look forward to their first day in your class.

Write a story about the time you accidentally broke your sister's favourite toy.

What is the worst food you have ever tasted? Describe it and explain why you did not like it.

If you could have lived in another century, would you? Explain your choice.

Write an account of a day that you will always remember.

What is the hardest thing you have ever done?

Write about an invention that you would like to see in your lifetime.

Describe your last visit to the dentist.

Think about some changes at your school that could make the days better.

Now, write a letter to the headteacher to persuade them that these changes are necessary.

If you were a super hero, what would be the first thing you would do?

Think of a time when you learned something difficult.
What was it? How did you feel?

Imagine you are alone on a desert island. Describe your experience.

What makes a good friend?

Write a story about the day you were the main character in a school play.

If you had three wishes, what would they be and why?

Write a story entitled "A day at the seaside".

Your cousin is travelling to your town by train. Write clear directions to help him get from the train station to your house.

Write a letter to your friends inviting them to a garden party at your home in the summer.

Describe your favourite hobby.

How is life in the 21st century different from when your grandparents were at school?

Write a description of someone you admire.

You have just bought a new rucksack and as you arrive back at home, you discover that it is faulty.

Write a letter to the shop manager explaining what the problem is and what you would like him to do.

Night is falling. Tom and Ben are still a long way from their tent ...

Continue the story.

"The day when everything went wrong".

Describe this day and how you felt.

Tom and Jack were on their way home from school. For the first time, they decided to walk across the field but somehow could not find their way back home. They were lost ...

Describe what happened.

Your teacher has just told the children that from next Monday, three aliens are going to join your class.

What do the children say? How do they feel?

Uncle Harry waited a long time at the bus stop. The bus was late and he only had an hour to get to the airport ...

Continue the story.

Tomorrow is 'Book Day' at your school. All the teachers and the children have been asked to dress up as their favourite character.

Who are you going to dress up as? Why have you chosen this character?

_____
_____
_____
_____
_____
_____
_____
_____
_____
_____
_____
_____
_____
_____
_____
_____
_____
_____
_____
_____
_____
_____
_____
_____
_____
_____
_____
_____

It had snowed a lot that morning. Holly decided to make a big snowman in the garden. She went briefly into the house to get an old hat and a scarf for the snowman, but when she got back into the garden the snowman was ...

Continue the story.

Have you ever won a prize in a competition? What competition was it and what was your prize? How did you feel?

Write a diary entry about how you felt when you went on a long journey by train.

What is your favourite television programme? Why do you like it so much?

Write an article for your school magazine explaining what we can all be doing to look after the environment.

What are the advantages of living in a big town?

Write a clear description of your favourite farm animal.

Write a letter to a friend who was unable to be with the rest of the class on a camping trip. Tell him what you enjoyed on the trip and also what you did not like.

Describe the view from your bedroom window.

Would you like to visit another planet? Give your reasons.

Write a story about a visit you make to some friends who live in a different country.

Describe how you help out at home.

If you could meet your favourite author, who would it be? What would you talk about? What questions would you ask him/her?

Write about a day in the life of a zoo keeper.

The plane landed safely at the airport. All the passengers cheered ...

Continue the story.

What is your favourite room in your house? Describe what it looks like and explain why it is the room you like best.

Write a letter to the headteacher to persuade him that all teachers at your school should also wear a uniform.

The moment the children arrived home, they shouted to their parents: "Look! Look what we have just seen!"

Continue the story.

You recently entered a competition and have just been notified that you have won the first prize.

What competition was it? What did you have to do? How are you feeling?

Imagine you are a traveller in a country you are visiting for the first time. Write about some of your adventures.

You are standing at a busy bus station on a cold Monday morning. Describe the scene.

You and your family are travelling by train to visit your grandparents. Write an interesting story about your day.

What do you think is the most valuable trait in a person's character?

Compare and contrast real school with virtual school.

What career would you like to pursue when you are older and why?

Describe a day in the life of a carpenter.

Describe a day of online-school during the coronavirus pandemic. Did you enjoy this school day? Why, or why not?

What is your favourite television programme?

Describe a visit to the farm.

Write about the advantages and disadvantages of living in a flat.

How can you encourage your family and friends to protect the environment?

Imagine you were allowed to paint any picture on your bedroom walls. What would you paint?

Write a letter to the Prime Minister telling him that you and your friends think that school holidays should be much longer and no school term should exceed ten weeks.

You have just moved to a new house and are exploring the attic. Describe what you find.

Bramley's Toy Company has just invented a new toy. The company wishes to let people know about the toy and produce an advertisement for local radio.

Write the words for the radio advertisement, to persuade people to buy the new toy.

Imagine a monster came over for supper. Describe the evening.

Imagine you are a £20 note. Tell me about a complete day in your life.

Printed in Great Britain
by Amazon